Songbirds

Jonathan P. Latimer
Karen Stray Nolting

Illustrations by Roger Tory Peterson

Foreword by Virginia Marie Peterson

Houghton Mifflin Company
Boston 2000

COLUSA COUNTY FREE LIBRARY

FOREWORD

My husband, Roger Tory Peterson, traced his interest in nature back to an encounter he had with an exhausted flicker when he was only 11 years old. When he found what he thought was a dead bird in a bundle of brown feathers, he touched it and the bird suddenly exploded into life, showing its golden feathers. Roger said it was "like resurrection." That experience was "the crucial moment" that started Roger on a lifelong journey with nature. He combined his passion for nature with his talent as an artist to create a series of field guides and paintings that changed the way people experience the natural world. Roger often spoke of an even larger goal, however. He believed that an understanding of the natural world would lead people — especially young people — to a recognition of "the interconnnectedness of things all over the world." The Peterson Field Guides for Young Naturalists are a continuation of Roger's interest in educating and inspiring young people to see that "life itself is important — not just ourselves, but all life."

— Virginia Marie Peterson

Copyright © 2000 by Houghton Mifflin Company
Foreword copyright © 1999 by Virginia Marie Peterson
All illustrations from *A Field Guide to the Birds* copyright © 1980 by Roger Tory Peterson and *A Field Guide to Western Birds* copyright © 1990 by Roger Tory Peterson

All rights reserved. For information about permission to reproduce selections from this book, write to Permissions, Houghton Mifflin Company, 215 Park Avenue South, New York, New York 10003. PETERSON FIELD GUIDES is a registered trademark of Houghton Mifflin Company.

The authors would like to thank Richard K. Walton, who reviewed and critiqued the manuscript, for his invaluable suggestions. Thanks also to Paul E. Nolting for his continued support and encouragement.

Library of Congress Cataloging-in-Publication Data
Latimer, Jonathan P. / Songbirds / Jonathan P. Latimer, Karen Stray Nolting; illustrations by Roger Tory Peterson; foreword by Virginia Marie Peterson. p. cm. — (Peterson field guides for young naturalists) Summary: Describes the physical characteristics, habitats, feeding habits, and voices of a variety of songbirds, arranged under the categories "Simple Songs," "Complex Songs," "Whistling Songs," "Warbling Songs," "Trilling Songs," "Name-sayers," and "Mimics."
ISBN 0-395-97941-2 (hardcover). — ISBN 0-395-97946-3 (pbk.)
1. Songbirds Juvenile literature. [1. Songbirds. 2. Birdsongs.] I. Nolting, Karen Stray. II. Peterson, Roger Tory, 1908– ill. III. Title.   QL696.P2L38   2000   598.8—dc21   9-38293 CIP

Photo Credits
All photos courtesy of the Cornell Lab of Ornithology. Cedar Waxwing: Isidor Jeklin; House Sparrow: Lang Elliott; Song Sparrow: Johann Schumacher; European Starling: Bob Schmitz; American Robin: Leslie McKim; Rose-breasted Grosbeak: Mike Hopiak; Northern Cardinal: J. R. Woodward; Northern Oriole: Mike Hopiak; Eastern Meadowlark: W. A. Paff; Common Yellowthroat: Isidor Jeklin; House Finch: Ted Tauceglia; Purple Finch: W. A. Paff; Warbling Vireo: Betty Darling Cottrille; Yellow Warbler: L. Page Brown; Chipping Sparrow: Mike Hopiak; Dark-eyed Junco: J. R. Woodward; Whip-poor-will: Bill Dyer; Black-capped Chickadee: Isidor Jeklin; Northern Mockingbird: James McCullough; Gray Catbird: Mike Hopiak

Book design by Lisa Diercks. Typeset in Mrs Eaves and Base 9 from Emigre.
Manufactured in the United States of America
WOZ 10 9 8 7 6 5 4 3 2 1

CONTENTS

HOW TO FIND SONGBIRDS

Songbirds are birds that communicate by singing. Over the years, people found some of these songs so pleasing that certain birds were nicknamed *songbirds*. For scientists, however, songbirds are part of a much larger group of "perching birds." The feet of these birds have three toes pointing forward and one back, which helps them grip a branch or twig when they perch. Scientists call this group *passerines*. It includes more than half of all the birds in the world. Songbirds such as finches, sparrows, thrushes, and warblers are passerines. Ducks, hawks, herons, and woodpeckers are not.

This book will help you recognize some of the songbirds you are likely to hear and see where you live. The book uses illustrations by the man who revolutionized bird identification, Roger Tory Peterson. He invented a simple system of drawings and pointers (now known as the "Peterson System") that call attention to the unique marks on each kind of bird. This book introduces the Peterson System to beginners and young birders. It can help you answer the most important question of all: *What kind of songbird is that?*

What Kind of Songbird Is That?

Many songbirds are easier to hear than they are to see, but sometimes you can follow their sound to find them. Also, you can learn to identify many birds just by hearing their song or call, even though they may be hidden from view. To make identification easier, the birds in this book are grouped by the type of song they sing.

The songs and calls of each bird are described in words, but those descriptions are only rough imitations. You can learn to identify songbirds best by listening carefully to the real sounds made by the birds around you. Once you see a bird, ask yourself the following questions to identify it.

What Color Is the Bird?

Color is one of the first things you notice when you see a bird. But color alone is not always enough. Many birds are the same color, or you may spot them in poor light, which makes the color hard to see.

Female Singers

Singing by female birds is less common in North America than in other parts of the world, but female cardinals and orioles can sing as well as males do. Pairs of cardinals are even known to sing duets.

Does It Have Any Field Marks?

The feathers of many birds have spots or stripes that will help you identify them. These are called *field marks.* Field marks can be found on a bird's head, wings, body, or tail. They can help you tell similar birds apart. In this book, useful field marks are pointed out on each illustration.

How Big Is the Bird?

Size is another quick clue to identifying a bird. Is it larger than a sparrow? Is it smaller than a pigeon? The size of the bird will help you exclude some choices and focus on others.

What Sound Does the Bird Make?

Songbirds make two kinds of vocal noises—songs and calls. They sound different and are used for different purposes.

A song is often long and complex. It is usually produced by males during the nesting season, but some females also sing. A song announces that a male has staked out his

territory and it warns other males to stay away. It also tells females that he is available as a mate. A song is often repeated over and over. After the spring nesting season, most males sing their song much less frequently.

Many birds can vary their song, often by making small changes in a basic pattern. A group of several songs or variations is known as a *repertoire*. A male cardinal has 8 to 12 songs in his repertoire.

A call is any of several shorter, simpler noises made by both males and females throughout the year. Calls are used for many things, including sounding alarms or keeping a flock together. Most young birds have special begging calls to tell their parents when they are hungry.

Does Each Bird Sing Its Own Song? Individual birds of the same species sing the same song, and each species seems to have its own song. Even closely related species sing differently. For example, a Song Sparrow can sing nearly 900 variations of its song. Its close relative, the Chipping Sparrow, sings one song over and over. A few birds, such as mockingbirds, can imitate the songs of other species. They are known as mimics.

When Do Birds Sing? You can hear birds singing most often in the early morning and the late afternoon. All songbirds sing more often in the spring nesting season than during the rest of the year. A few even sing in winter.

Where Do Birds Sing? Many songbirds sing from the highest perch they can find. On open grasslands where there are no high perches, birds such as meadowlarks often sing while they hover high above their nesting sites. These songs are called *flight songs*.

How Do Birds Learn Songs? Some birds seem to inherit their songs directly from their parents, with little learning involved. Other birds learn their songs by listening to their parents. These young birds begin by warbling meaningless notes, like the babbling of a human baby. Gradually they combine these sounds into fragments of song. After much practice, a young bird learns to sing the songs of its species properly.

How Do Birds Sing? Birds have an unusual box at the bottom of their windpipe called a *syrinx*. This box is controlled by muscles. A bird pushes air through the syrinx and the muscles make it vibrate. This vibration produces sound.

Keeping Track
Many people keep a list of all the birds they have ever seen. This is called a Life List. You can begin yours with the list on page 48. It includes all the birds described in this book.

CEDAR WAXWING

You seldom see just one Cedar Waxwing. They usually travel in flocks that suddenly appear on a tree or hedge and feed on its berries. They are sociable birds that signal each other with a buzzy call that sounds like *zeee*. Cedar Waxwings sometimes sit side by side on a branch and pass a berry up and down the line until one of them swallows it. They can be gluttons too, eating so many berries that they can barely fly.

Cedar Waxwings have a special way of feeding their young. The parent swallows as many as 30 berries, holding them in a pouch in its throat, called a crop. When it returns to the nest, it feeds these berries to its young one at a time.

Did You Know?

- Cedar Waxwings get their name from the fact that they love cedar berries and because the feathers of their wings produce a bright red waxy substance.
- During nest-building Cedar Waxwings may take yarn or string from a person's hand.

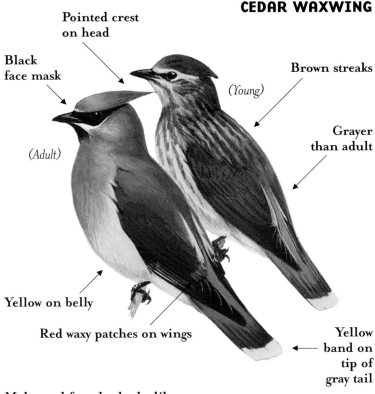

Pointed crest on head

Black face mask

(Young)

Brown streaks

Grayer than adult

(Adult)

Yellow on belly

Red waxy patches on wings

Yellow band on tip of gray tail

Males and females look alike.

Cedar Waxwings are almost always seen in groups.

Habitat Cedar Waxwings are found around trees and shrubs that contain berries, especially along the edges of forests and streams. They may also be seen in parks or in suburban gardens.

Voice A high, thin, buzzy *zeee, zeee.*

Food Cedar Waxwings eat all kinds of berries, including juniper, dogwood, and cedar. In summer they also eat insects that they catch in midair. They may come to feeders for raisins or currants.

HOUSE SPARROW

Even though they are considered songbirds, House Sparrows don't sing very well. Their song is a series of unmusical chirps, but House Sparrows have a large vocabulary of calls. To us, their call sounds like a scolding chatter, but at least 11 different types have been identified. Each call seems to have a distinct purpose. Some are warnings, with separate calls for different dangers. Others are used to keep the flock together or to signal when they have found food.

House Sparrows can be seen in most cities. They seem fearless when they approach people for food scraps. Sometimes they are hard to identify because they are coated with soot, which hides their true colors.

Did You Know?

• House Sparrows are not native to North America. Around 1850 a small number were released in Brooklyn, New York. This flock spread quickly and by 1900 House Sparrows could be found throughout the United States and southern Canada.

• The House Sparrow is also known as the English Sparrow.

Gray stripe on head

Light cheeks

Black throat

(Female)

Buff color line over each eye

(Male)

No streaks on chest

Habitat House Sparrows have been very successful in living with people. They find themselves at home in cities and on farms, but they are rarely found in woods or other undeveloped areas.

Voice The most common sound made by a House Sparrow is *cheep, cheep.*

Food House Sparrows eat mainly seeds, but in the warmer months they eat many kinds of bugs. They have even been known to eat insects off the grilles of parked cars. House Sparrows also eat scraps and crumbs left by people and will visit bird feeders.

SONG SPARROW

These little brown birds are found throughout North America, but they look different in different places. In the North they are darker and larger. In the deserts of the Southwest they are smaller and paler. One thing is certain—you can always identify Song Sparrows by their bright, cheery songs.

Young Song Sparrows learn their songs by listening to other Song Sparrows sing. But how well they learn these songs seems to depend on timing. Young Song Sparrows must hear the songs at a particular time—from about 10 days after hatching to about 50 days after. If a young Song Sparrow does not hear the songs of its species during that time, it is never able to learn them.

Did You Know?

- Song Sparrows are one of the most common native birds. They can be found as far north as Alaska and as far south as Mexico.
- Each Song Sparrow has three or four songs it sings regularly, but most start with three or four sharp notes.
- During one 24-hour period a Song Sparrow spent 9 hours singing, 9 hours sleeping, and 6 hours eating or on other activities.

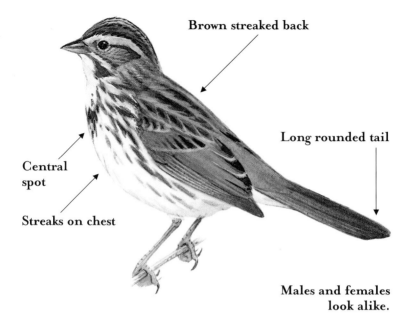

Brown streaked back

Long rounded tail

Central spot

Streaks on chest

Males and females look alike.

Song Sparrows pump their tails as they fly.

Habitat In most places Song Sparrows are found in brush or thickets near water and in gardens with heavy bushes or shrubs. Along the coast they are found near the edges of salt marshes.

Voice The song of the Song Sparrow can contain both musical and buzzy notes. It often starts with 3 or 4 piping notes that sound like *sweet, sweet, sweet.* These are followed by various notes and trills.

Food Song sparrows eat seeds and many kinds of beetles, grasshoppers, caterpillars, ants, wasps, and spiders.

STARLING

A starling is a loud black bird with a long bill and a short tail. Its harsh, grating *tseeeer* sound or whistling *whooee* are hard to miss. Starlings make many other sounds as well, including whistles and clicks. They also imitate other bird calls and even barking dogs or mewing cats, though not nearly as well as mockingbirds.

Starlings live almost everywhere people do. Tough and aggressive, they are chunky birds that look like black triangles when they fly. In fall and winter, flocks of starlings can be seen wheeling through the sky. They twist and turn in perfect precision although there does not seem to be any leader. Sometimes hordes of starlings cause serious damage to fruit crops. These flocks break up when nesting season begins.

Did You Know?
• It is estimated that there are as many as 200 million starlings in the United States and Canada.
• Winter flocks of starlings and other birds have been estimated to be as large as 10 million birds. They are noisy and messy and nearly impossible to drive away. Attempts to disperse them with chemicals, loud speakers, gun shots, or by destroying their habitat have been mostly unsuccessful.
• The starling's official name is European Starling.

Heavily speckled

Dark bill

Gray-brown

Shimmering feathers

Yellow bill

(Young)

(Winter)

(Summer)

Short square tail

Males and females look alike.

Habitat Starlings can be found on farms and in cities and towns. They also live in parks and on open fields.

Voice Starlings make many sounds, including a harsh, grating *tseeeer* sound. They also imitate other bird calls.

Food Starlings hunt for a wide variety of insects in grass and on the ground. In fall and winter, flocks of starlings and other birds eat large quantities of insect pests such as weevils, cutworms, grasshoppers, and Japanese beetles.

ROBIN

The song of the robin is a series of clear caroling notes that rise and fall in pitch. This song can often be heard at dawn or dusk and can last a long time. Robins also call with a short *tyeep* or a *tut-tut*.

Robins hunt by sight. In spring and summer you can often see them running or hopping on lawns. They often stop and stand upright, looking for insects and earthworms in the grass.

A robin's nest is made of twigs and mud and is shaped like a cup. Both parents feed their chicks and will defend their nest vigorously. When baby robins can fly, the male takes over their care. The female then begins a second nest.

Did You Know?
• Robins build their nests wherever there are trees or shrubs for support and mud for nesting material.
• Some robins spend winter in the North. They stay in woods where they can find food.
• The robin's official name is American Robin. It is the state bird of Connecticut, Michigan, and Wisconsin.

Yellow bill

Dark gray back

Colors slightly paler than male's

Speckled breast with rusty-colored background

(Young)

(Female)

Red breast the color of bricks

(Male)

Habitat Robins live in cities, towns, and forests. They hunt for food on lawns, farmland, and open meadows.

Voice Robins sing in the early morning during spring and summer. Their song is a series of caroling notes that sounds like *cheerily, cheer-up, cheerily.*

Food In spring and summer robins eat mostly insects and earthworms, which they also feed their young. In fall and winter they eat mostly fruits and berries.

GROSBEAKS

The songs of grosbeaks are among the most beautiful of any bird song. Both males and females sing a rising and falling song that was described by Roger Tory Peterson "as if a robin has taken voice lessons." Male grosbeaks sing to attract a mate in spring, but they sing throughout the year as well. Males and females share the responsibility for caring for their young, and some males have even been heard singing while sitting on their nest.

Grosbeaks are about the size of starlings. They get their name from their large, strong bills, which they use to crack open nuts and seeds. The Rose-breasted Grosbeak is found mainly in the East and the Black-headed Grosbeak in the West, but their territories overlap in the Midwest.

Did You Know?
- Grosbeaks help farmers by eating pests that attack their crops, such as potato beetles.
- Grosbeaks eat all kinds of seeds and berries. They even eat the berries from poison oak. If you touched those berries, you might get an itchy rash.

Rose-breasted Grosbeak

Black and white pattern on back and wings

Large rose-red triangle on chest

Striped head

Streaks on chest

(Female)

(Male)

Rust color on neck and chest

(Female)

Black and white on wings

Light stripes on head

Yellow on chest

(Male)

Black-headed Grosbeak

Habitat Grosbeaks are usually found in oak forests, especially in open areas such as the edges of fields or along streams. They migrate to the tropics in winter.

Voice The songs of both grosbeaks are similar to the robin's, only mellower and more flowing. They are rich, whistling songs that can last a long time. Both also call with a sharp, metallic note that sounds like *kik* or *eek*.

Food In summer, grosbeaks hunt many kinds of insects, including beetles, caterpillars, bees, and flies. They also eat many kinds of seeds and berries throughout the year. Grosbeaks will come to bird feeders for seed.

CARDINAL

You may hear a cardinal long before you see the brilliant scarlet red feathers of a male. Listen for a short, thin *chip* that seems to come out of the undergrowth. That is the call of a Northern Cardinal. They also have several songs, which are longer. Like many birds, Northern Cardinals can vary their song, often by making small changes in a basic pattern.

The male Northern Cardinal is the only red bird with a crest of feathers on its head found in North America. Female Northern Cardinals also sing, but they are a little harder to spot than the males. Females are brown or olive-gray, and their wings and crests are edged in red. Both males and females have thick red bills.

Did You Know?

• A male Northern Cardinal can sing 8 to 12 songs.

• When cardinal chicks leave the nest, the male takes care of the first brood while the female lays another set of eggs. She may lay as many as 4 broods in a single season.

• The cardinal's official name is Northern Cardinal. It is the state bird of more states than any other bird. They are Illinois, Indiana, Kentucky, North Carolina, Ohio, Virginia, and West Virginia.

Thick triangular red bill

Black face patch

Bright red pointed crest

Like female but with black bill

Red edge on crest

(Young)

Red bill

(Female)

(Male)

Habitat Cardinals live year-round in dense underbrush along the edges of fields or woods, or in parks. During winter you may see flocks of cardinals numbering as many as 60 or 70 birds.

Voice The cardinal's song is a whistle that often sounds like it is saying *what cheer, what cheer,* or *wheat, wheat, wheat,* or *pret-ty, pret-ty, pret-ty.* They also make a short, sharp call that sounds like *chip.*

Food You can see cardinals hopping around on the ground or moving through shrubs or trees looking for food. They eat a wide variety of bugs, including caterpillars, beetles, grasshoppers, and even slugs. Cardinals also eat fruits and wild seeds. At a bird feeder they will eat sunflower seeds and cracked corn.

ORIOLES

Orioles are among the most beautiful songbirds of North America, and they build one of the most intricate nests. It is a deep pouch that hangs from a drooping branch. It is woven by the female, with occasional help from the male, out of plant fibers, hair, yarn, or string.

Then it is lined with grass or other soft materials. The orioles enter their nest through a small opening at the top. Although they are similar, the nest of a Baltimore Oriole is often deeper than the nest of a Bullock's Oriole.

People once thought that the Baltimore Oriole and Bullock's Oriole were really one species. However, they have different patterns of feathers and different songs, and they live in different places. Today they are considered two separate species.

Did You Know?
- The Baltimore Oriole was named in honor of Cecilius Calvert, known as Lord Baltimore, who founded Maryland in 1632. It is the state bird of Maryland.
- Bullock's Oriole was named after William Bullock, an English traveler who brought the first specimens to London from Mexico in 1823.

Baltimore Oriole

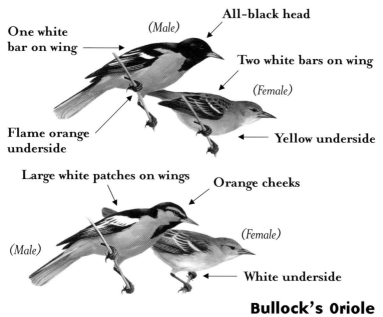

One white bar on wing

(Male)

All-black head

Two white bars on wing

(Female)

Flame orange underside

Yellow underside

Large white patches on wings

Orange cheeks

(Female)

(Male)

White underside

Bullock's Oriole

Habitat Baltimore Orioles are found in the East and Midwest. Bullock's Orioles are found mainly in the West. Both orioles are found in open woods and groves of shade trees. They seem to favor elm trees. They spend winter in the tropics.

Voice The song of the Baltimore Oriole is a clear, rich whistle that sounds like a flute. It also calls with a low whistle that sounds like *hew-li*. Bullock's Oriole sings a series of double notes with 1 or 2 piping notes. It calls with a sharp *skip* or sometimes a chatter.

Food In summer, orioles eat mostly insects, including caterpillars, beetles, and grasshoppers. They also eat berries, fruit, and the nectar from flowers. They will sometimes take sugar water from hummingbird feeders or can be attracted with orange halves.

MEADOWLARKS

Eastern and Western Meadowlarks are both chunky birds that have a black V on their bright yellow chests. In fact, they look so much alike that hearing them is often the best way to tell them apart. Their beautiful songs are totally different. A Western Meadowlark sings 7 to 10 gurgling notes that sound like a flute. The song of an Eastern Meadowlark is a clear whistle that sounds like *tee-yah, tee-yair.* Their calls are also different.

Meadowlarks sing throughout the year, even in winter and during migration. Males often perch atop fence posts in open fields or along roads and sing. When a meadowlark takes off, it flashes a patch of white feathers on each side of its short, wide tail.

Did You Know?
• Female meadowlarks build their nests by weaving dried grasses and plant stems together. The nest is shaped like a dome and has a small entrance on one side.
• The Western Meadowlark is the state bird of Kansas, Montana, Nebraska, North Dakota, Oregon, and Wyoming.

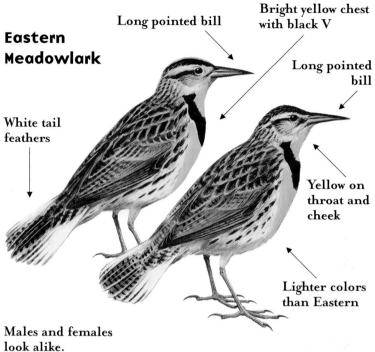

Eastern Meadowlark

Long pointed bill

Bright yellow chest with black V

Long pointed bill

White tail feathers

Yellow on throat and cheek

Lighter colors than Eastern

Males and females look alike.

Western Meadowlark

Habitat Meadowlarks can be found all year in fields, meadows, and prairies.

Voice The Eastern Meadowlark has a musical 2-note song. Its call is a rasping or buzzy *dzrrt*. The Western Meadowlark has a 7- to 10-note song that sounds like a flute. Its call is lower than the Eastern Meadowlark's and sounds like *chupp*.

Food Meadowlarks eat many kinds of insects, particularly grasshoppers, crickets, and beetles. They also eat seeds and grain.

COMMON YELLOWTHROAT

These brightly colored little warblers can be found near almost any marsh or stand of cattails during spring and summer. The Common Yellowthroat is the only warbler in North America that nests in these wet areas. Their cheerful song is unmistakable, but they are usually scarce where the land is dry.

The nest of the Common Yellowthroat is large for such a small bird. It is a bulky cup made of grass anchored to the vegetation around it. Unfortunately, this nest is very attractive to cowbirds. Cowbirds are parasites that lay their eggs in other birds' nests. The original nest-builders end up losing their young and taking care of the baby cowbird. Common Yellowthroats are one of the most frequent victims of cowbirds.

Did You Know?

- The Common Yellowthroats' behavior of darting from place to place reminds many people of wrens.
- Common Yellowthroats migrate mostly at night. They spend winter in swampy areas as far south as Panama.

Black mask

Olive-brown back

(Male)

(Female)

Bright yellow throat

Whitish underside

Females and young look alike.

Habitat Common Yellowthroats are found most often in marshes and other swampy areas with thick brush. They also nest in moist thickets and tangles of weeds near water.

Voice The song of the Common Yellowthroat is a bright, rapid chant that sounds like a rolling *witchity–witchity–witchity–witch* or *witchy–witchy–witchy–which*. It also calls with a raspy *tchep*.

Food Common Yellowthroats hunt many kinds of insects and bugs, including grasshoppers, dragonflies, beetles, grubs, caterpillars, moths, and ants. They also eat spiders and occasionally seeds.

HOUSE FINCH

Listen for the bright warbling song of these lively red and brown birds in your backyard. Their song often ends in a harsh nasal *wheer* or *che-urr*. House Finches are frequent visitors to bird feeders and seem to have little trouble adapting to humans. Some finches even build their nests on the high ledges of buildings or in holes in telephone poles.

Male House Finches may sing at any time of year. They sometimes perch on high places and sing for long periods. Females sing during spring. House Finches are social birds and often appear in small groups, although they sometimes gather in large flocks. They tend to return to the same nest year after year.

Did You Know?
• House Finches are very adaptable. They are native to the western United States, but in the 1940s some were released in Long Island, New York. Since then they have expanded across the entire United States.
• House Finches will hang on a hummingbird feeder and drink the sugar water.

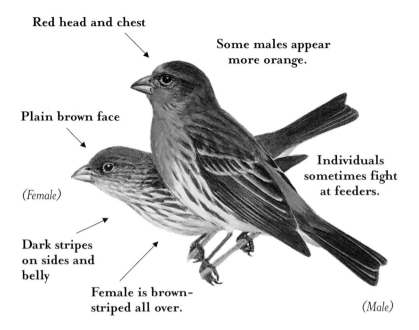

Red head and chest

Some males appear more orange.

Plain brown face

(Female)

Individuals sometimes fight at feeders.

Dark stripes on sides and belly

Female is brown-striped all over.

(Male)

Habitat House Finches have adapted to a wide range of environments. They live on farms and in towns and cities. They are familiar backyard birds and easily adjust to the presence of people.

Voice House Finches have a long, high-pitched warble. The song ends in a harsh and slurred *wheer* or *che-urr.* Their call is a sweet *cheep,* similar to a House Sparrow's but more musical.

Food House Finches seem to be able to eat almost anything. In the country they eat primarily seeds, but in cities they will search the streets for crumbs and food scraps. House Finches flock to bird feeders. They will eat a variety of seed, including sunflower and thistle seeds.

PURPLE FINCH

Although it is called "purple," a male Purple Finch is really a rich rose color, especially on its head and rump. Roger Tory Peterson described the male Purple Finch as looking "like a sparrow dipped in raspberry juice." It can be mistaken for a House Finch, but its fast, lively warble helps tell them apart. The song of the Purple Finch is clearer and does not end in the harsh *wheer* or *che-urr* like that of a House Finch.

> **Did You Know?**
> • As they fly, Purple Finches sometimes make a call that sounds like *tick* or *tuck*.
> • The Purple Finch is the state bird of New Hampshire.
> • Purple Finches migrate in flocks. They travel mostly during the day.

In the past, Purple Finches were one of the most common birds found at bird feeders. Today, however, they are seen less often, probably because of the competition from House Sparrows and House Finches. You may see Purple Finches at a feeder or searching for food high in trees.

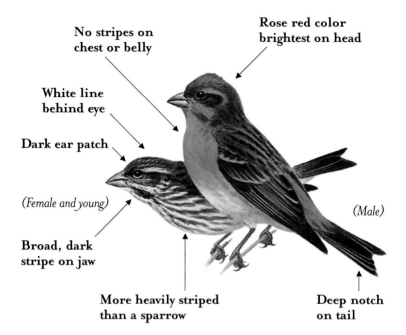

No stripes on
chest or belly

Rose red color
brightest on head

White line
behind eye

Dark ear patch

(Female and young)

(Male)

Broad, dark
stripe on jaw

More heavily striped
than a sparrow

Deep notch
on tail

Habitat Purple Finches are most often found along the edges of woods or groves of trees, but they can also be seen deep in the woods. In winter they can be seen in almost any wooded area.

Voice The song of the Purple Finch is a fast warble that sometimes ends abruptly. Their dull, metallic call note sounds like *tick.*

Food The main food of Purple Finches is seed, including seed from trees such as ash or elm. They also eat berries and the buds from plants in spring. In summer they eat some insects and caterpillars. At a bird feeder they will eat sunflower seeds.

WARBLING VIREO

During spring and summer the song of the Warbling Vireo is often heard in wooded gardens or parks. Like other vireos, a Warbling Vireo repeats its song over and over. It sings throughout the day, even in the heat of midday when most other birds are quiet.

This plain little bird can often be seen searching for insects or bugs along branches of trees or shrubs. It hops along twigs and pokes among the leaves with its bill. It may also hover and pick insects off the bottoms of leaves.

Warbling Vireos hide their nests high in trees. The cup-shaped nest hangs by its rim from a forked twig. You may not see a nest, but you might hear a male Warbling Vireo singing while he sits on it.

Did You Know?
- Vireos are found only in the Americas.
- Warbling Vireos are usually seen alone or in pairs. They rarely form flocks.
- Warbling Vireos migrate as far south as Central America each year.

Olive-green back and wings often look gray

White eyebrow stripe

Bill slightly hooked

White chest

Vireos look like warblers but are less active.

Males and females look alike.

Habitat Warbling Vireos are found in wooded areas, especially in shade trees near the edges of woods or along streams. They are often found around elms or aspens, but they usually avoid deep woods.

Voice The song of the Warbling Vireo is a long continuous warble. It sounds like a Purple Finch but is less lively and slower. It sometimes is described as sounding like *brig-adier, brig-adier, brigate* with the last notes rising in pitch. Their wheezy call sounds like *twee.*

Food Warbling Vireos eat mostly insects, including beetles, ants, flies, and dragonflies. They also eat caterpillars and some spiders and snails. In late summer and fall they eat many kinds of small berries and fruits, including sumac, elderberry, and poison oak.

YELLOW WARBLER

The Yellow Warbler is one of the easiest warblers to spot in summer. It is the only bird in North America that looks all yellow at a distance.

Yellow Warblers are often victims of cowbirds. Cowbirds are parasites that lay their eggs in the nests of other birds and let them raise the young cowbirds. But when a female Yellow Warbler notices a cowbird's egg among her own, she quickly buries it by creating a new bottom for her nest. Unfortunately she also buries her own eggs and must lay new ones. One Yellow Warbler's nest was found to have 5 layers of buried eggs, each with a cowbird egg. This Yellow Warbler finally beat the cowbird, however, by laying a sixth group of eggs and raising her own young.

Did You Know?
- Male Yellow Warblers usually hunt insects higher up in trees than females.
- Yellow Warblers in different areas specialize in hunting different insects. Yellow Warblers in Nebraska eat lots of grasshoppers. Those in Massachusetts eat gypsy moths.

Yellow stripes on tail

Sharp, pointed bill

Yellow all over

Yellow stripes on tail

(Female)

(Male)

Rust-colored streaks on chest

Yellow Warblers are smaller than House Sparrows.

Habitat Yellow Warblers are most often found in woods or thickets near water. They can be seen along the edges of streams and lakes and in swamps and marshes.

Voice The song of the Yellow Warbler is a cheerful, bright *sweet, sweet, sweet, little more sweet.* They also call with a loud *cheep* or a buzzy *zeet.*

Food Insects make up most of the diet for Yellow Warblers, including flies, moths, mosquitoes, grasshoppers, and beetles. Yellow Warblers also eat some berries.

CHIPPING SPARROW

These little sparrows get their name from the bright chipping sound of their song. You will often hear a Chipping Sparrow singing before you see it. They spend much of their time on the ground looking for food in grass or in the litter beneath trees. Chipping Sparrows can be found in gardens and yards throughout North America.

Chipping Sparrows were once known as the "hairbird" because they plucked hairs from horses to line the inside of their nests. As cars replaced horses, Chipping Sparrows had to find other materials. Today they line their nests with grass, but they will use hair if they can find it. They have even been seen plucking hairs from sleeping dogs.

Did You Know?
- Male Chipping Sparrows sometimes sing at night.
- Although it was one of the most common birds found in towns during the nineteenth century, in many places it has been replaced by the House Sparrow, which was introduced from Europe in the 1850s.

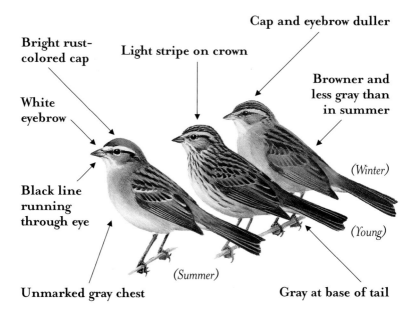

Cap and eyebrow duller

Bright rust-colored cap

Light stripe on crown

Browner and less gray than in summer

White eyebrow

(Winter)

Black line running through eye

(Young)

(Summer)

Unmarked gray chest

Gray at base of tail

Males and females look alike.

Habitat Chipping Sparrows once lived mostly in pine forests, but today they are found in gardens, city parks, orchards, and on golf courses and farmland.

Voice The song of the Chipping Sparrow sounds like a rattle. Its call is a dry *chip.*

Food During most of the year Chipping Sparrows eat seeds, especially those from grass or weeds. During summer they eat mostly insects, caterpillars, and grasshoppers.

DARK-EYED JUNCO

Juncos are known as "snowbirds" because they appear in most places when the weather turns cold. In spring they nest in the northern parts of the United States and Canada or stay high in the mountains, where it remains cool.

There are several different juncos found in North America, but those with dark eyes are all considered one species. In different places Dark-eyed Juncos are known as Northern Juncos, Oregon Juncos, and Slate-colored Juncos.

Except during nesting season, juncos gather in small flocks. These flocks have a "pecking order." This means that some birds in the flock rank higher than others. In junco flocks, the pecking order determines where a bird can look for food. If you see juncos fighting, the contest is usually about rank.

Did You Know?
- The same flocks of juncos return to an area year after year.
- Juncos find seeds on the ground by scratching in the snow or leaves.

Slate-colored Junco

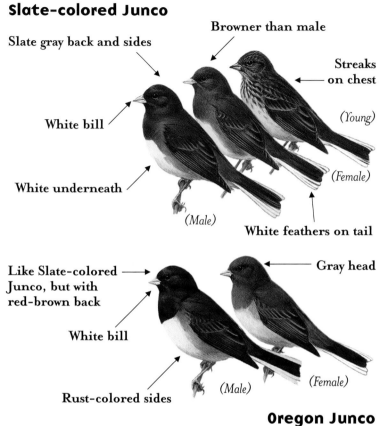

Browner than male

Slate gray back and sides

Streaks on chest

(Young)

White bill

White underneath

(Female)

(Male)

White feathers on tail

Like Slate-colored Junco, but with red-brown back

Gray head

White bill

Rust-colored sides

(Male)

(Female)

Oregon Junco

Habitat Juncos live at the edges of forests near meadows or other open spaces. They can also be found in patches of brush and along roads. In some places they live in parks and yards.

Voice Juncos have a sweet, musical trill. They also use a scolding call that sounds like *smack*.

Food Juncos eat seed and grain. During nesting season they may also eat insects. They will come to a bird feeder, but they usually eat the seed scattered by other birds on the ground below the feeder.

WHIP-POOR-WILL and POORWILL

At dusk on a summer night you may hear a Whip-poor-will repeat its name over and over. In fact, this is a bird you may hear but never see. It hunts in the forest during the night, catching insects, especially moths, in its gaping mouth and swallowing them whole. During the day it sleeps on the forest floor where its brown feathers blend with the color of fallen leaves.

Whip-poor-wills are found primarily in the eastern half of North America. In the West you are more likely to hear the poorwill, which also says its name. It is thought that the name "poorwill" comes from the Hopi language and means "the sleeping one." A poorwill can stay in a deep sleep for days or even weeks at a time.

Did You Know?
- Someone once counted as one Whip-poor-will repeated its call more than 1,000 times.
- Poorwills hibernate during cold weather. Whip-poor-wills migrate south for winter.
- The official name of the poorwill is Common Poorwill.

Whip-poor-will

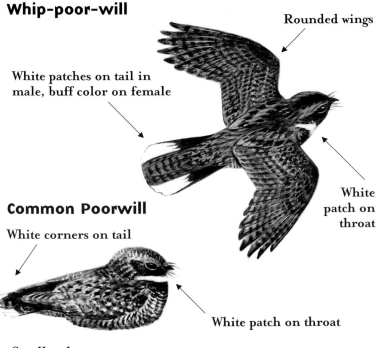

Rounded wings

White patches on tail in
male, buff color on female

White
patch on
throat

Common Poorwill

White corners on tail

White patch on throat

Smaller than a
Whip-poor-will

Stiff whiskers may be used
to detect insects in dark.

Males and females look alike.

Habitat Whip-poor-wills are found in dry forests.
Common Poorwills are found in dry hills or open brush
with scattered shrubs.

Voice The Whip-poor-will repeats its name about
once a second with a definite rhythm—*whip-poor-will.*
The Common Poorwill repeats a loud, whistled *poor-will*
or *poor-jill-ip.*

Food Both Whip-poor-wills and Common Poorwills
eat moths and other insects, which they often catch in the
air. They also eat beetles, grasshoppers, and mosquitoes.

BLACK-CAPPED CHICKADEE

Chickadees practically identify themselves. Their clear call of *chick-a-dee-dee-dee* rings through woods or thickets. Sometimes they cut their call down to a sharp *dee-dee-dee*, which may sound angry or like a warning. Often you will hear an answering call from another chickadee nearby. Occasionally they mix high-pitched notes or sputters with their calls. If a female Black-capped Chickadee is dis-

turbed on her nest, she may hiss like a snake.

Chickadees can be seen all year. They often call at bird feeders, zooming in to pick up a seed, and then flying away. Sometimes they will perch on a branch to eat the seed, but they also store seeds in cracks in tree bark for later. In the woods chickadees are often found with other small seed eaters such as finches or sparrows.

Did You Know?

- Chickadees spend almost as much time hanging upside down on branches and bird feeders as they do right-side up.
- A male and female make their nest in a hole in rotten wood or in an old woodpecker hole. The pair digs the hole together.
- The Black-capped Chickadee is the state bird of Maine and Massachusetts.

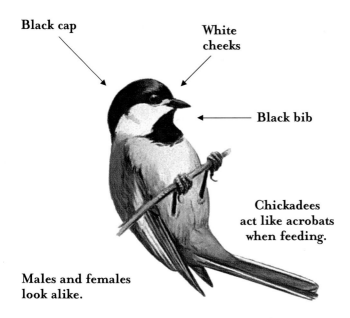

Black cap

White cheeks

Black bib

Chickadees act like acrobats when feeding.

Males and females look alike.

Habitat Look for chickadees in wooded areas or in trees and shrubs near houses.

Voice Chickadees get their name from the call they make. Listen for their cheery-sounding *chick-a-dee-dee-dee* throughout the year. Their song is a clear whistle that sounds like *fee-bee-ee* or *fee-bee*.

Food Chickadees eat mostly insects, seeds, and berries. At bird feeders they especially like sunflower seeds and suet.

MOCKINGBIRD

Mockingbirds are the best bird mimics in North America. One was heard imitating the calls of 32 different birds in just 10 minutes. They are so good that they can even fool the birds they are imitating. How Northern Mockingbirds learn another bird's song is a mystery, but it is known that they can learn new sounds throughout their lives.

Mockingbirds are not just mimics—more than 80 percent of their songs are original. Some have been known to sing more than 150 different songs. A male mockingbird may sit on a high perch and sing all day or all night, especially in moonlight. They often repeat the same song over and over, sometimes making small changes in it as they sing.

Did You Know?
- The mockingbird's official name is Northern Mockingbird. It is the state bird of Arkansas, Florida, Mississippi, Tennessee, and Texas.
- A Northern Mockingbird will repeat its song over and over.

Longer tail than a robin's

White patches on wings

White patches on tail

Males and females look alike.

Habitat Mockingbirds are usually around all year. They are found in towns, on farms, and along roadsides.

Voice Mockingbirds make a wide variety of sounds, even copying croaking frogs, barking dogs, or the sound of a squeaky wheelbarrow. Their call is a harsh *tchack* or *chair.*

Food During spring and summer Northern Mockingbirds hunt for insects while walking or running on the ground. In fall and winter they eat mostly berries and other fruit.

GRAY CATBIRD

Like mockingbirds, Gray Catbirds are also excellent imitators. In fact, their name comes from their call, which sounds like a cat mewing. Catbirds can imitate jays, hawks, chickens, and even tree frogs.

Catbirds spend much of their time looking for food on the ground, stirring through dead leaves with their bill. They often make quite a bit of noise, and you may hear a catbird rustling leaves before you see it. Although its feathers are very plain, it can be identified by the way it flips its tail as it moves around.

Gray Catbirds are very inquisitive and can become quite tame. In the North they will stay throughout winter if there is a supply of food. In the South they stay year-round.

Did You Know?

- You can attract Gray Catbirds by imitating their mewing call. They will come to investigate, often unexpectedly popping out of a shrub or hedge.
- Gray Catbirds are rarely seen in flocks. They live alone or in pairs during nesting season.
- Gray Catbirds will come to feeders for an unusual variety of foods, including peanuts, crackers, doughnuts, and even corn flakes.

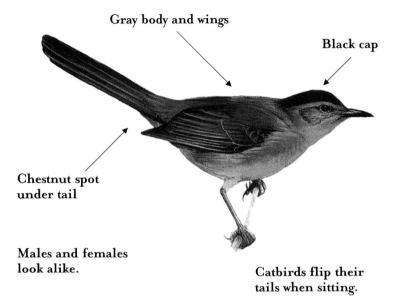

Gray body and wings

Black cap

Chestnut spot under tail

Males and females look alike.

Catbirds flip their tails when sitting.

Habitat Gray Catbirds are usually found in dense undergrowth, particularly in thickets along the edges of woods or streams. They also can be found in hedges in gardens and overgrown brushy fields.

Voice The mewing call that sounds like a cat is easy to recognize, but catbirds also imitate the songs of other birds. Unlike mockingbirds, catbirds usually do not repeat a song over and over. Catbirds also make a grating call that sounds like *tcheck–tcheck*.

Food In spring and summer Gray Catbirds hunt through the undergrowth for many kinds of insects, especially beetles, grasshoppers, and crickets, as well as caterpillars, spiders, and millipedes. They also eat many kinds of berries.